GAUGUIN

Gauguin

Text and Notes by
PAUL C. NICHOLLS

TUDOR PUBLISHING COMPANY
New York

TUDOR PUBLISHING COMPANY

New York, 1967

Library of Congress Catalog Card Number: 67–19836

Printed in Japan

GAUGUIN, REBEL PAINTER

An aura of romance has long surrounded Gauguin's life, veiling the truth behind the image of the noble savage. Several recent publications have tended to dispel this by emphasizing his adherence to Western tradition even in the remote South Seas. The glowing aesthetic achievement of his pictures, however, remains unchallenged.

Gauguin is remembered chiefly for his pursuit of primitive life in Brittany, Panama, Martinique and Polynesia. His arrogance and conceit, his inclination to self-pity, were eclipsed by the boldness of this highly significant adventure. For although his particular quest for the primitive was typical of a general interest at the time in returning to the origins of art, and his fugitive retreat to Polynesia symptomatic of a widely felt despair with European civilization, his exploits hastened the first real appreciation of primitive art. Further, his unconventional use of accepted media expanded the range of art beyond the confines of the Beaux-Arts tradition.

There were irreconcilable conflicts within this rebel. In his life, he aspired to acclaim and renown but defiantly pretended to despise the public and refused to conform—the savage at once rejected but superior. In his art, too, his professed contempt for rules concealed an interest in aesthetic theory on the expressive effects of line, form, and color. Thus, without making any consistent formulation, he strove to achieve emotive effect through the simplification of form and the arbitrary use of color.

Another feature of his style is the habit of "visual quotation" and borrowing from the works of several painters, including Degas, Puvis de Chavannes, Cézanne and Manet, as well as from a number of photographs. "He is always poaching on someone's ground," Pissarro once exclaimed, "now he is pillaging the savages of Oceania." His intent, it seems, was to produce a confluence of associations within the same picture. Also, figures and poses in his own paintings become images impregnated with special significance to be repeated in later pictures. Frequently they serve to suggest an *idea* rather than any explicit allegory or event. As he once told his friend de Monfreid, "In painting one must search rather for suggestion than description, as is done in music. Sometimes people accuse me of being incomprehensible only because they look for an explicative side to my pictures that is not there."

THE FIRST PHASE

We know little of Gauguin's early life. Born in Paris on June 7th, 1848, the infant Paul was taken to Peru in 1851, because his father feared the political turn of events in France. When his father died on the journey, his mother continued with Paul and his sister to Lima. After four years they returned to Paris and settled in Orléans.

His penchant for the exotic can partly be explained by his early association with strange cultures, although his claims to savage Peruvian ancestry can be discounted as mere pretension. Little is known of the years spent in naval service from 1865–71, but his sea voyages set a pattern for the roving adventure of his whole life.

The person who guided and informed his early artistic tastes was Gustave Arosa, stockbroker, art collector and photographer. On the death of Gauguin's mother, Aline, in 1867, Arosa became his guardian. In the two years before his marriage, Gauguin lived with Arosa in a home containing a large collection of pictures and photographs, many of which appear in Gauguin's own work (see Note 69).

Through Arosa, Gauguin obtained a position as a stockbroker and began work in 1871 at Bertin's bank. Here he met Émile Schuffenecker, a fellow stockbroker and also an amateur painter, who remained a loyal friend for long after. By 1873 his success on the Bourse qualified him as an approved match for a well-bred Danish girl, Mette Sophie Gad, whom he married in November that year.

The problem of when Gauguin first ventured into painting is not fully resolved. At any rate, the evidence is clear that he had already begun oil painting in the early 1870s. In 1874, the year which witnessed the birth of his first child, Émile, Gauguin became a regular Sunday painter and occasionally went to the Atelier Colarossi with Schuffenecker to draw from a model. His early painting style partakes strongly of the Barbizon School tradition, recalling particularly Corot and Daubigny.

Sometime during 1875 his style was fertilized by a meeting with the kindly Pissarro, who taught Gauguin, as he did Cézanne and Van Gogh, the Impressionist technique. Through Pissarro he also made the acquaintance of other Impressionists, who met at the Café de la Nouvelle-Athènes in Paris. Toward 1880, with the profits accruing to him from speculation on the Bourse, he began to amass a collection including works by Manet, Pissarro, Renoir and Degas, and some admired Cézannes.

To the Fifth Impressionist Exhibition of 1880 Gauguin submitted several landscapes in Pissarro's style. The next year he entered a wooden statuette, a painted plaster medallion and seven pictures, including *Study of a Nude* (3). Thus he firmly allied himself with the new group. However, his presence there was not well received by all; Monet for one did not approve of the membership of "any dauber that comes along." Open dissension within the group at this time merely emphasized the divergence of their artistic aims, which became increasingly apparent in the 1880s. Gauguin was gradually attracted away from the *plein-air* Impressionism of Pissarro and Monet toward Manet and Degas, whose attention was focused more on pictorial interest than on the recording of transient visual phenomena (2). He played an important part in the reaction against Impressionism of the 1880s by utilizing the color experiments of Impressionism for the description of an inner vision, a subjective reality, in new pictorial terms (8).

PAINTING FULL TIME

By 1883 he felt the attraction of a full-time career as a painter too strongly to continue with his job at the bank. From this point on his financial troubles began and soon multiplied. Early the next year, against the better judgment of Pissarro, he moved from Paris to Rouen, in the mistaken hope of finding cheaper lodgings for his family and a better market for his paintings. His failure in both reduced his capital considerably and embittered his relations with Mette, who viewed his "metamorphosis" with utter dismay. She eventually left for Denmark in August, but returned in October when Gauguin agreed to go and live with her in Denmark.

In Copenhagen he attempted to sell tarpaulins for a French company, but this proved as fruitless as his one-man exhibition at the Society of the Friends of Art, which failed to receive any recognition in the press. His inefficacy made him an object of ridicule and contempt in the eyes of Mette and her family. Finding this intolerable, and being disgusted generally with the complacent primness of the Danish bourgeoisie, he left with his son Clovis for Paris in the summer. In the bitter winter of 1885–86 which ensued, he was forced to work as a bill-poster, while Mette, more vindictively than helpfully, resorted to selling pictures from his prized collection.

Some of the artist's personal relationships with other painters suffered during this miserable period. During a stay at Dieppe in 1885, he quarreled with Degas, and in the following year fell out with Seurat. The latter quarrel was aggravated by his jealousy of Seurat's rising reputation. Seurat had conspicuously broken with Impressionist tradition, and Gauguin felt that Seurat had stolen his role as the new Messiah. He began to attack and ridicule the "divisionism" of the Neo-Impressionists, among them his master Pissarro.

SEARCH FOR THE PRIMITIVE

Under these circumstances, what could have been more natural than his decision to go to Brittany in late June of 1886? There, new subjects were to be found, steeped in folklore; and furthermore, he had been informed of a cheap inn—the Pension Gloanec in Pont-Aven—where credit was extended to painters. Contrary to Gauguin's opinion, the majority of painters who frequented this increasingly popular artist's retreat were not influenced by him, and even opposed his revolutionary principles, although his impact on the colony was considerable notwithstanding. Gauguin met here Charles Laval, who accompanied him to Panama in the following year, and Emile Bernard, a young man who was to be instrumental in the transformation of his style two years later.

On his return to Paris in November he tried his hand at ceramics, but as a commercial venture this too failed. Also, physical illness obliged him to spend most of December in a hospital.

Wearying of misfortune, he announced to Mette in early April, 1887, his intention of going to live as he said, "like a savage," in Panama; and somehow scraping together enough money, set sail with Laval later the same month. His sister, on whose hospitality in Panama he had counted, gave him a poor reception. He rapidly became disillusioned with the Indians and caught dysentery and yellow fever in the bargain. The adventure would have ended ingloriously if Gauguin had not decided to disembark at Martinique on the return journey. On this lush island Gauguin completed twenty paintings in four months, capturing in full the brightness of tropical color and the poetic mystery of the ponderous forms of the Negress (7). But their exhibition by Theo van Gogh at Goupil's gallery in January resulted in only three sales.

Dispirited by yet another failure, Gauguin again set off to Brittany. Among the detached group which centered around Gauguin there was Émile Bernard, who, being intellectually curious and well versed in the literary ideas then current in Paris, acted as foil to the older man, stimulating and perhaps clarifying Gauguin's ill-formed theories. Bernard brought with him some canvases done in St. Briac, which had been greatly admired by the critic Aurier. He later insisted that his pictures inspired Gauguin's *Vision after the Sermon* (8) and the style of "Synthetism," which aimed at gaining more forceful expression through simplification of pictorial form. The dispute eventually provoked bitter animosity between the two.

In fact, Gauguin's new style owed much both to the flat simplicity of the Japanese print and to a technique, devised by Bernard's friend Louis Anquétin, known as "cloisonnism," which had been inspired by stained glass. However, in his ceramics Gauguin had already reduced his designs to simple shapes and outlines, and as regards the new theory itself, a letter to Schuffenecker of January 14th, 1885, two years earlier, had already outlined a synthetist program in suggesting that simplicity of form might transmit immediacy of sensation.

In October, Gauguin finally took up a frequently expressed invitation from Van Gogh to join him in Arles. They had met originally in November, 1886, and formed a friendship on the strength of their enthusiasm for painting. Now in Arles wide differences in temperament underlined those in their art. Van Gogh preferred to paint from nature, Gauguin from memory. Van Gogh admired Daumier, Daubigny, Ziem and Theodore Rousseau, but disliked Ingres, Raphael, and Degas, all of whom Gauguin admired. Gauguin continued to paint Breton themes in Arles, but a noticeable lightening of his palette occured and his touch became livelier. He later made unjustified claims to having radically influenced Van Gogh's style, which admittedly showed a temporary change; but from the preceding it is clear that Gauguin himself benefitted from his stay. After the well-known tragedy of the last days of 1888, Gauguin returned to Paris.

In Paris he set about organizing an exhibition of painters of his own choice, designed to enter the Exposition Universelle of 1889 by the back door. It was entitled "Groupe Impressioniste et Synthétiste" and covered the walls of a café at the exhibition run by a proprietor named Volpini. Accountable as a failure as far as the public was concerned, it nonetheless served Gauguin's purposes in furthering his leadership of a small following and in bringing to the notice of the Symbolists, especially Félix Fénéon, Gustave Kahn and Aurier, a style which they were soon to find conveniently illustrative of their own ideas.

Gauguin was fascinated by certain parts of the Exposition Universelle itself. He was particularly delighted with some of the Far Eastern displays, which included a Javanese village complete with dancing girls. Another interesting section showed the Evolution of the Dwelling. The whole Exposition whetted his appetite for the primitive; and he made several drawings.

In the early summer Gauguin drifted back discontentedly to his Brittany haunts to nurse the seeds of revolution. There he first stayed at the Pension Gloanec in Pont-Aven, but later moved to the inn run by Marie Henry at Le Pouldu, the dining room of which he and his disciple-friends decorated with paintings and carvings. The religious theme of several of his pictures at this time (20, 21, 22) was suggested by some of Aurier's writings and also by Bernard's devout Catholicism. But the image of himself as Christ symbolized not only a sense of martyrdom but also a Messianic hope fostered now by the attentions of his disciples at the inn, and later by the Symbolists in Paris.

During his stay at Arles, Gauguin had enjoyed a successful one-man show at Theo van Gogh's gallery in Paris, but later in 1889 Theo's enthusiasm waned noticeably and with it Gauguin's chances of selling. A reason for this is that Gauguin's style in 1889 lacked consistency and firm ideological foundation. The outlines softened and the stark simplicity of cloisonnism was modified by a reversion to Cézannesque modelling. He wavered between pictures inspired by Breton subjects (18, 20) and others less conventional (24, 35) whose unusual themes invited acclaim by the Symbolists, particularly Aurier. However, the latter demurred despite pressure from Bernard, and apart from an article in *La Cravache* by Fénéon, not entirely favorable, Gauguin remained without recognition. At an exhibition with "Les Vingt" in Brussels he was even mocked openly, while both Theo and Degas increasingly expressed dislike for his latest pictures.

We learn with little surprise, therefore, that he applied, albeit abortively, for a colonial post in Tonking with the hope of tapping the art and philosophy of the Orient. In Paris early next year conversations with Mme. Redon, who had visited Madagascar, suggested this as an alternative. Émile Bernard, one of the group whom Gauguin planned to take, had meanwhile unearthed the romantic novel on Tahiti by Pierre Loti, as well as an official handbook on Tahiti. On reading these Gauguin's mind was resolved.

The charms of this fabled isle had beguiled many a voyager before Gauguin. Its special attraction for him was the promise of a cheap and carefree life, unfettered by the chains of progressive materialism and as free from constraint in art as in sexual morality. But another consideration expanded further the opportunities Tahiti offered: new subject matter. Van Gogh had first pointed out the commercial attraction of the hitherto unpainted tropics, but it was the Symbolists who alerted his attention to other aspects. After another spell in Brittany during the summer, he had returned to Paris in November to find a reputation at last secured for him among the Symbolists by two of his Brittany students. He was introduced to these admiring literary circles by Aurier. However, witness accounts indicate that his rough and ready theories fell so ill on their refined ears that he prudently decided to profit from exploiting their ideas rather than attempting to preach his own. A number of themes were current in their discussions: the *rêve*, mystery, decadence and pessimism, all with a common source in Baudelaire. They also sighed over Europe and dreamed of faraway isles. Gauguin needed no introduction to Baudelaire, whose admiration for Delacroix he shared, but the preoccupations of the Symbolists certainly enlivened his own ideas, and the mysterious enchantment of Tahiti promised to be fertile in the essential material of Symbolist art.

In order to obtain funds for a ticket, Gauguin organized a sale of his paintings and applied for an "official commission" to the Minister of Education. In both he was successful; the sale at the Hotel Drouôt in late February received massive publicity from the Symbolists, especially from Octave Mirbeau, whose lengthy article in *L'Art Moderne* already began to spin the threads of myth about the artist. With Mette, Gauguin fondly made amends during a brief trip to Copenhagen in March, with the agreement to resume married life on his return in three years' time. The Symbolists celebrated his departure with a farewell dinner on March 23rd, and a week later, on April 1st, 1891, he set sail.

TAHITI

His first impression of Tahiti was bound to be disappointing. European influence had spread to every part of the capital, Papeete, and although he was happy to enjoy high social status on account of his official commission, he failed to discover the fabled glamor of his dreams. By degrees he gravitated to the less respectable levels of Tahitian society, and his portrait commissions ceased when the strange style of his first portrait became known. After three months he wearied of the capital and withdrew to the country, still hoping to find the ancient culture of Tahiti unspoiled. His departure was delayed by an internal hemorrhage, symptomatic of an advanced syphilitic condition.

But even in the country the marvels of civilization had replaced the ancient crafts, just as Christianity had effaced the ancient religion (60). Through a lucky acquaintance with an amateur painter, he gained access to the remoter region of Paea, where *Man with an Axe* (40) was painted. After his return to Papeete he set out for the district of Mataiea, which provided sufficient new subjects for him to complete about twenty pictures in which a happy mood predominates (33, 37, 38).

Gauguin had come to Tahiti with naïve preconceived ideas about the "native life." As a consequence he tended to idealize his surroundings to the extent of believing in the magic world he created on canvas. His ideal savage splashed in the lagoons, hacked fruit down from the trees and hunted game in the forests. Unfortunately, without the necessary skill in obtaining native foods, he had to buy what he could from a local store. Furthermore, his sophisticated tastes in drink meant that in spite of his cheap bamboo hut, life was not cheap. He therefore sought to earn money from a post as magistrate in the Marquesas Islands and on refusal, wrote to France for repatriation in June 1892. It was granted a year later.

During the delay he sought to satisfy a deeply felt need for a female companion. He had soon tired of Titi, a girl of the city whom he sent back to Papeete.

Eventually he found a young girl named Teha'amana, who was offered and wedded to him in true Tahitian style. In Tahitian women generally he found not beauty, but "a sort of fascination, something infinitely mysterious." Teha'amana, wth a countenance as innocent as Eve's, helped him make believe in his garden of Eden. She steadied him and revived his strength.

His early pictures idealized Tahiti. With masterful simplicity and colors more glowing than ever, he described an idyllic environment; but he felt that reference to native folklore and tradition was lacking. He interpreted a Christian theme in Tahitian terms (34) but the discovery in 1892 of J. A. Moerenhout's account of ancient Tahitian mythology released a stream of new ideas. From this he abstracted certain sections and compiled them with illustrations in a volume entitled *L'Ancien Culte Mahorie.* This supplied the basic material both for the book he wrote later called *Noa Noa* and for several pictures (e.g., 45), woodcuts (53), and woodcarvings begun in late 1892 (91, 92, 93, 94). This material certainly was not provided by Teha'amana, as he relates in *Noa Noa,* since he hardly mastered enough Tahitian even to converse with her.

Both the painter and his pictures found a mixed reception in Europe when he returned in 1893. In Copenhagen the Free Exhibition of Modern Art was well attended but made few sales. Theo's old gallery, now under new management, refused to handle his pictures, forcing him to seek exhibition at the Galérie Durand-Ruel. Some of his most celebrated pictures (34, 45, 47) were greeted with derision and abuse. Only eleven of the 44 exhibits were sold. A heavy heart and light purse persuaded him to flee Europe for good, but with hope still of success he began to collaborate with the poet Charles Morice on *Noa Noa,* a book designed to help the public understand his Tahitian pictures. For this he executed ten superb woodcuts (53).

His fortunes took a brief turn for the better in 1894 when he finally suceeded in obtaining a legacy of 13,000 francs from an uncle in Orléans. Of this he spitefully sent Mette only a fraction; altercations had begun again over money matters in which it seems neither was honest. His new wealth enabled him to afford a new mistress, a young half-caste called Anna (55) resembling the Javanese girls he had admired at the 1889 Exposition Universelle.

In April, 1894, he returned with Anna for his last and ill-fated trip to Brittany. On an excursion to Concarneau he and his companions became involved in a brawl with some sailors, during which he broke his right ankle. While he was recovering

13

and in some pain, Anna deserted to Paris and rifled his studio of all but the pictures. As if this were not enough, his case against Marie Henry, for the illegal retention of some of his paintings, failed. He therefore resolved to escape again to the South Seas, this time for good.

As for the first trip, he arranged a sale of his pictures to raise money. But despite his ingenious tactic of obtaining publicity by the publication of a letter from Auguste Strindberg in the preface of the catalogue, he sold only nine out of forty-seven pictures. His departure was further delayed by another syphilitic attack, which impaired his health for several months.

RETURN TO POLYNESIA

On route he touched at Sydney and then Auckland before arrival at Papeete, now so civilized he immediately proposed to travel on to the remoter Marquesas Islands. He remained, however, because his poor health required proximity to Tahiti's hospital, and built a hut for himself in Punauia with carved wooden panels and posts. His new sores frightened away Teha'amana, but he soon found a new mate, Pau'ura (69).

At first he spent recklessly, and as funds ran out another syphilitic attack and the recurrence of pain from his ankle increased his misfortune. His ailments restricted his painting activity and required at first painkilling drugs and then hospital treatment. This last enabled him to resume work by the end of October and he modelled some clay statues for his garden. Financial support from Paris gave him a brief period of happiness. Two magnificent works of this period (71, 72) were despatched to Paris by cruiser. Then, in April, 1897, news came of the death of his favorite daughter, Aline.

Not long after, the death of his landlord obliged him to move to a new house, on which he lavished sums of money outside his means. In a period of acute unhappiness, when money troubles again coincided with severe illness, he wrote *The Modern Spirit and Catholicism*, a confused metaphysical discussion containing an attack on the Catholic Church. His mood of increasing unhappiness came to a climax at Christmas, 1897: after painting his pessimistic philosophy on a monumental canvas (68) he attempted suicide with arsenic.

The story of the rest of his stay in Polynesia is marked by the recurrence of illness and debts. The latter obliged him to take a job in the Public Works Department in Papeete until a large sum of money arrived in January 1899 from the faithful de Monfreid. Eventually he was able to live in moderate comfort when the dealer Vollard agreed, in March, 1900, to pay a regular monthly allowance. In the years 1898–9 Gauguin indulged in a spate of political activity with attacks on the natives and the administration, even to the point of fining and imprisoning Pau'ura. He appears to have become rapidly disenchanted with the Edenic idealism of his earlier days there. After publishing articles in *Les Guêpes*, a monthly newspaper of the Catholic party, he founded his own magazine, *Le Sourire*, in August, 1899, as the mouthpiece of attacks against the administration.

In 1900 he carried out his original intention of moving to the Marquesas. There, beyond the range of colonial officials, in a more barbaric environment, the cost of living, and of models, was less high. He hoped still to immerse himself in the ancient culture, and anecdotes in *Racontars de Rapin*, a book he wrote there, strongly suggest that he did. However, it is more likely that, as in *Noa Noa*, he described more what he hoped to see than the truth. At the same time, despite the rude aspects of his house on Atuona, he took pains to secure the comforts of civilization for himself. But he also increased his output of paintings, and in some the mystery of a remoter region is evoked by subtle imagery (78, 79).

The erotic activity which took place in his "House of Pleasure" aroused friction between Gauguin and the local authorities, a friction which, rebellious to the last, he exploited, ultimately to his own disadvantage. In particular he antagonized the local bishop with a satirical wooden sculpture. Some of his renewed attacks on the administration, in his role as defiant champion of the natives, are recorded in a mischievous collection of memoirs and anecdotes entitled *Avant et Après*.

His attacks recoiled on him. On March 31, 1903, the local magistrate fined him 500 francs and sentenced him to three months imprisonment for libel against a gendarme. The strain of trying to obtain legal redress for this unjust sentence, together with the rapid deterioration of his health, brought about his death at the age of 55 years.

Toward the end of his life Gauguin felt a desire to return to Europe, and in a letter to de Monfreid mentioned Spain as a possible source of new subject matter. De Monfreid warned him against this: "You must not return. Now you are as are the great dead. You have passed into the history of Art." To de Monfreid he also personally confided his estimation of his own achievement: "You have known for a long time what it has been my aim to vindicate: the right to dare anything . . . The public owes me nothing since my pictorial oeuvre is only *relatively* good, but the painters of today who are benefitting from this new-won freedom do owe me something." This statement, made in a moment of rare modesty, is confirmed by the bold experiments in technique and use of materials made throughout his work; it is contradicted by the testimony of countless of his canvases in which subtle design is combined with unparalleled coloristic splendor.

PAUL NICHOLLS

Brief Bibliography

Wildenstein, G.: *Gauguin, sa vie, son oeuvre.* Paris, 1958. (Gazette des Beaux-Arts publication.)

Chassé, C.: *Gauguin et son temps.* Paris, 1955.

Danielsson, B.: *Gauguin in the South Seas.* London, 1965.

Gray, C.: *The Sculpture and Ceramics of Paul Gauguin.* Baltimore, 1963.

Gaugin, Paul: *Lettres de Gauguin à sa femme et à ses amis.* Edited by M. Malingue. 2nd ed. Paris, 1949.

Gauguin, Paul: *Noa Noa.* Trans. by J. Griffin. Pub. by Cassirer, 1961. (Recommended for the information it contains on the different editions of the original, and also because facsimile copies are not readily available.)

Rewald, J.: *Post-Impressionism.* New York, 1962. (2nd ed.) (Contains important information on Gauguin and an annotated bibliography.)

Wildenstein, G.: *Gauguin, Vol. I. Catalogue.* Paris, 1964. (Main catalogue of illustrations. But see also the review in *Burlington Magazine,* Jan. 1966, by M. Bodelsen.)

PAUL GAUGUIN

1848–55   Born in Paris, June 7, 1848. In 1851, is taken to Peru when his father decides to emigrate because of the political situation. Father dies on the journey, mother and two sisters continue to Lima. In 1885, family returns to France and settles in Orléans.

1865–71   Goes to sea as a sailor in the French navy. Gustave Arosa becomes his guardian on the death of his mother. On release from navy, takes up stockbroking at Bertin's Bank, where he meets Émile Schuffenecker.

1873–75   By now has begun to paint, encouraged by Schuffenecker and assisted by his guardian's daughter. Marries Mette Sophie Gad in November, 1873. In 1875, meets Pissarro. Begins to form collection of Impressionist painters.

1880–82   Exhibits at the 5th, 6th and 7th Impressionist Exhibitions.

1883–86   Resigns job at Bertin's to paint full time. Moves to Rouen as resources run low. Mette leaves for Denmark in August, 1883, and Gauguin follows in December. Works as agent for tarpaulin manufacturers. In summer 1885, returns to Paris with son Clovis. Works as bill poster during the winter. First visit to Brittany in summer of 1886. Stays at Pension Gloanec.

1887–88   Determines to live like a savage in Panama. Leaves with Laval April 10th. Contracts dysentery and yellow fever. Stops off at Martinique on return journey. In 1888, exhibits Martinique pictures at Goupil's Gallery. Returns to Brittany in summer of 1888. In fall, visits Van Gogh at Arles, returning to Paris after Van Gogh tries to attack him on Christmas Eve.

1889–90   Exhibits with Les Vingt in Brussels. Visits Exposition Universelle. Summer in Brittany. Tries to get post in Tonking. During 1890, the Symbolists take him up. Considers going to Madagascar or Tahiti.

1891–93   First Tahiti Period. Leaves France on April 4th. Lives in Papeete with a *vahine* called Titi, first of several native paramours, several of whom will bear him children. Moves to Mataiea after severe illness. In 1892, money troubles oblige him to seek repatriation, which he obtains in May, 1893. During this period, he is inspired by native colors and forms, paints, makes sculpture. Exhibition at Galerie Durand-Ruel, Paris, in November. Begins writing and making woodcuts for *Noa Noa*.

1894–95   Breaks and infects ankle in Brittany in the spring. Javanese mistress leaves him. Resolves to return to South Seas for good. After another attack of syphilis and a disastrous sale at Hotel Drouot, sets sail, planning to settle in the Marquesas. Stays at Punauia, Tahiti, instead, to be near hospital.

1896–97   Second South Seas Period begins. Syphilitic eruptions and unhealed ankle cause almost incessant pain. Money troubles also plague him, despite remittances by his friend de Monfreid and dealer Vollard. Contracts double conjuntivitis. Attempts suicide in 1897. In 1898, works in Office of Public Works. In 1899, money from de Monfreid enables him to spend lavishly, but debts soon recur. Begins continued attacks on the natives and the administration.

1900–01   Vollard buys his entire output, providing a monthly allowance in return. In winter, Gauguin is again hospitalized, with skin infection and influenza. In August, 1901, sails for the Marquesas because of rising living costs. Arrives at Atuona, Hivaoa, September 16. Constructs "House of Pleasure."

1902–03   Spends extravagantly on food and wine. Mentions returning to Europe. In 1903, continues attacks on the administration. Skin infection and eyesight trouble frequently prevent him from painting. Found guilty of libel, fined and sentenced to 3 months in prison. Dies while planning appeal, May 8.

NOTES ON THE COLOR PLATES

1. *Gauguin Before his Easel*. 1885. Oil. Private Collection, Berne. Now a fully-fledged painter, Gauguin expertly handles the Impressionist technique acquired from Pissarro's instruction. His participation in three Impressionist exhibitions has established his reputation as a painter.

2. *Still-Life in an Interior*. 1885. Oil. Private Collection, U.S.A. Gauguin plays with pictorial ambiguity in the use of double perspective in foreground and background, and in the introduction of a border on the extreme left of the wall. The background scene thus appears as a painting of a mirror reflection or of an actual painting (cf. 69).

3. *Study of a Nude*. 1880. Oil. Ny Carlsberg Glyptotek, Copenhagen. Exhibited at the sixth Impressionist Exhibition in 1881, this picture was greatly admired by Huysmans, who praised the vitality and realism of the skin. Gauguin, he said, was the first for years to try to represent the woman of his day. It is very much in the tradition of Courbet.

4. *The Beach at Dieppe*. 1885. Oil. Ny Carlsberg Glyptotek, Copenhagen. The bright atmosphere of the coast attracted many painters because it offered great opportunities for intensive study of effects of color and light. Gauguin's approach is considerably influenced by Pissarro and Monet.

5. *Cows by the Seaside*. 1886. Oil. Private Collection. Gauguin became thoroughly absorbed in the ruggedness of Brittany, which he visited for the first time this year. The cows and the Breton girl, incidental figures in the whole, serve to give the scale of the picture.

6. *Four Breton Women*. 1886. Oil. Bayerische Staatsgemäldesammlungen, Munich. The strange shapes of the native costumes fascinated Gauguin. This

picture exhibits a marked flatness; all three visible faces are seen in profile and the omission of details of their feet leaves their exact location in space uncertain. Very similar motifs were used in Gauguin's first ceramics begun in the winter of 1886–7.

7. *Two Women from Martinique.* 1887. Charcoal and pastel. (Present whereabouts unknown.) This is the fruit of Gauguin's first quest as a painter to the tropics. The simple sketch is a perceptive description of the ponderous form of the Negress.

8. *Vision After the Sermon* or *Jacob Wrestling with the Angel.* 1888. Oil. National Gallery of Scotland, Edinburgh. Gauguin explained his magnum opus of 1888: "The scene witnessed by these women, most of whom kneel down in prayer, represents an apparition that occurred to them after hearing the Sunday sermon in their village church." The red field on which the action takes place and the strangely diminutive cow impart an air of unreality. The flatness of the composition, the large areas of relatively unmodelled color reveal its formal connection with Japanese prints and the indirect influence of cloisonné technique. The painting marks the birth of "synthetism" and a radical break in Gauguin's style. He told Schuffenecker: "This year I have sacrificed all, execution and coloring for style, intending to compel myself to do something different from what I usually do."

9. *Still-Life with Three Puppies.* 1888. Oil. Museum of Modern Art, New York. In this enigmatic picture Gauguin daringly combines a Cézannesque still-life with motifs probably inspired by a print of Kunyioshi. It may represent an attempt to paint in the manner of a child, a prelude to deliberate primitivism in Tahiti. Gauguin once expressed his wish as a painter to return to the "rocking-horse" of his childhood.

10. *Landscape with Cows.* 1889. Water-color. Private Collection, New York. The extremely foreshortened shapes of the cows are nicely accommodated within the overall flatness of the whole.

11. *Les Alyscamps, Arles.* 1888. Oil. The Louvre, Paris. The weft of

small strokes, in many areas consistently painted parallel to the diagonal, clearly shows Gauguin's attempt to utilize a technique patiently elaborated by Cézanne. The latter even accused Gauguin of trying to steal what he called his "petite sensation." The bright light and intense color of Arles contrast with the pearly gray light of Brittany.

12. *Woman with Pitcher, Pont-Aven.* 1888. Oil. Private Collection, New York. An intensely personal orchestration of colors in Gauguin's interpretation of typical Brittany landscape. Relatively naturalistic pictures like this form the basis for more imaginative "abstract" works (17).

13. *Old Women of Arles.* 1888. Oil. Art Institute of Chicago. This subject was also painted by Van Gogh, with whom Gauguin stayed in Arles. Gauguin's version uses large areas of relatively unmodulated color, and the handling of the paint surface is far less excited. Most noticeable is the exaggerated inclination of the background, bringing it well within the picture plane, as in a Japanese print. The ground level perspective of the gate acts as a foil to the otherwise high viewpoint.

14. *Among the Lilies, Brittany.* 1889. Oil. Kunstmuseum, Basle. The dog is copied directly from a Courbet that was once in the collection of Gauguin's guardian, Gustave Arosa. It occurs again elsewhere (30, 75). Gauguin often used the same figure in several compositions, sometimes reversed.

15. *Haymaking.* 1889. Oil. Courtauld Institute of Art, London. This is one of two such scenes painted in July at Pont-Aven. The powerful sweep of the composition from bottom left to the center, emphasized by the direction of many small brushstrokes, is expressive of the subject. An unusually gay picture in a year of extreme discontent.

16. *La Belle Angèle.* 1889. Oil. The Louvre, Paris. The sitter, Mme. Angèle Satre, was keeper of a local café. She was not allowed to see the portrait until it was finished, at which time she expressed her utter horror. Theo van Gogh, on the other hand, singled it out for praise on account of its fresh and countrified effect. He compared the composition of the portrait with "the big

heads in Japanese crêpons." The Peruvian idol has been explained as a vindictive caricature of Mme. Satre's husband, but may simply reflect Gauguin's love of exotic objects.

17. *Women Gathering Seaweed.* 1889. Oil. Folkwang Museum, Essen. The seated figure on the right, used elsewhere as a symbol of melancholy (68, 73), gives the picture an air of desolation keenly felt by Gauguin at the time. The schematic treatment of the figures harks back to a painting made by Émile Bernard in August, 1888, which Gauguin exchanged for one of his own paintings.

18. *Young Breton Girls by the Sea.* 1889. Oil. National Museum of Western Art, Tokyo. These girls are portrayed in traditional Le Pouldu costume. The stance of their disproportionately large feet gives them an awkward attitude. Paradoxically, sentimental appeal, strongly evident in this picture, is a quality Gauguin pretended to deplore.

19. *Still-Life with Fan.* 1889. Oil. The Louvre, Paris. Some parts of the picture, the knife, tablecloth and apples, are an almost literal transcription of a Cézanne in Gauguin's possession. In the background is a design for a fan and to the right a pot, unknown as a separate ceramic.

20. *The Green Christ.* 1889. Oil. Musées Royaux des Beaux-Arts de Belgique, Brussels. Gauguin has made use of a Romanesque stone carving, the Calvaire of Nizon, near Pont-Aven. The sombre colors produce a melancholy effect and the obvious echoing of the form of the stone Christ in the lines of the peasant indicates strong symbolic overtones. The gloomy nature of the picture recalls Gauguin's words to Schuffenecker: "I love Brittany. I find wildness and primitiveness there. When my wooden shoes ring on this granite, I hear the muffled, dull, and powerful tone which I try to achieve in painting."

21. *Christ in the Garden of Olives.* 1889. Oil. Norton Gallery and School of Fine Art, West Palm Beach. Gauguin saw himself as a painter-messiah, and attempted to gather a band of disciples of his own in Brittany. Depressed and filled with a sense of betrayal, he painted this self-portrait in the image of Christ, in which the central tree sets him pictorially apart from the traitor Judas, his

other disciples already having left him to the agony of Gethsemane. An unfortunate inclination towards self-pity no doubt induced Gauguin to use this obvious symbolism.

22. *The Yellow Christ.* 1889. Oil. Albright-Knox Art Gallery, Buffalo. This is the third of the three pictures done in the autumn of 1889 based on the Passion of Christ (20, 21, 22). The figure of Christ, derived from a wooden polychrome crucifix in the chapel of Tremalo, near Pont-Aven, again symbolizes Gauguin's own suffering, while the figures in the distance, quickly disappearing once prayers are done, as Mirbeau interpreted them, may perhaps be compared to the allegorical background of the previous picture.

23. *Self-Portrait with the Yellow Christ.* 1889. Oil. Private Collection. The mirror image of the Yellow Christ and the picture of one of his own self-portrait pots, made from a photograph, add strong emotive effect to this searching self-portrait.

24. *Self-Portrait as a Symbolist.* 1889. Oil on wood. National Gallery, Washington, D.C. The halo, the serpent, and the apples, are signs of a preoccupation with Satanism. The painting style, bordering on caricature, owes much to the simple boldness of the Japanese print and the rich intensity of cloisonnism.

25. *Still-Life with Ham.* 1889. Oil. Phillips Gallery, Washington, D.C. In this simple but forceful still life, the solid three-dimensional objects on the table-top are held in pictorial balance by the emphatic verticals of a two-dimensional background.

26. *Still-Life with Japanese Print.* 1889. Oil. Private Collection, New York. In this bright still-life Gauguin combines a Japanese print and one of his own self-portrait pots made in Peruvian style. The rhythmic disposition of the elements in broad horizontal bands may be compared with (37). Gauguin's interest in the Japanese print was as much for its association with the contemplative philosophy of the East as for the new pictorial schema it provided.

27. *The Schuffenecker Family.* 1889. Oil. The Louvre, Paris. Gauguin

met Schuffenecker as a fellow banker at Bertin's in 1871. Also a painter, he often entertained Gauguin at his house and helped him even after they became estranged, in 1891, on account of Gauguin's improper conduct toward Mme. Schuffenecker.

28. *Madeleine Bernard*. 1888. Oil. Musée des Beaux-Arts, Grenoble. In a pensive portrait, we see the woman for whose affections Gauguin competed unsuccessfully with Laval. The dancers' feet on the wall behind explicitly confirm the inspiration of Degas in this portrait. Degas in turn admired and collected a number of Gauguin's pictures.

29. *Les Folies de l'Amour*. 1890. Gouache. Private Collection. The rounded shape suggests that this may have been a design for a plate. The theme of love is playfully presented in an accumulation of esoteric symbols.

30. *Harvest by the Sea*. 1890. Oil. Private Collection, London. See Note 35.

31. *Nirvana: Portrait of Meyer de Haan*. 1889. Oil and turpentine on silk. Wadsworth Atheneum, Hartford. Nirvana was also Schopenhauer's solution to the problems of life, and something of his pessimism, to which Gauguin inclined, is captured in the extraordinary brooding and melancholy of this portrait. The woman with raised hands is an old-age and death figure (cf. 68) and the rocks, Les Roches Noires, had special associations in local folklore. This stylization of de Haan's features is used again in (79) for the evocation of mood.

32. *The Field of Potatoes*. 1890. Oil. Private Collection, New York. This transposition of a simple rustic subject into a field of magically bright colors looks forward to the gayness of Gauguin's early Tahitian pictures.

33. *Two Tahitian Women on the Beach*. 1891. Oil. The Louvre, Paris. These bronzed Tahitian figures were apparently both inspired by the same model, a local inhabitant who has posed here in two different positions. Their thoughts appear to be united in pensive meditation (compare the two figures in 63).

Gauguin was fully sensitive to the amplitude of their languid forms, and something of the carefree delight which he took in his new wife and primitive surroundings is felt in the radiant colors of his early Tahitian pictures.

34. *Ia Orana Maria.* 1891. Oil. Metropolitan Museum of Art, New York. Finding the ancient Tahitian religion virtually extinct, Gauguin interpreted Christian themes in Tahitian terms: "Ia Orana Maria" is the Tahitian "Ave Maria." The figures assume poses derived from a frieze of the Javanese temple of Borobodur, of which Gauguin had photographs.

35. *The Loss of Virginity.* 1890–91. Oil. Chrysler Art Museum, Provincetown. See also Plate 30. The landscape background of (30) clearly forms the setting for (35). The difference lies in the increased stylization of the second picture, appropriate to its symbolic intentions and heightened by the expressive effect of its emphatic horizontality. Gauguin reproved Puvis de Chavannes for his excessively literary symbolism, but as the fox is Gauguin's "Indian symbol of perversity," and the plucked flower the stock symbol of the loss of virginity, the picture seems to contradict his own criticism. More in keeping with his professed intentions is the evocative effect of simplified colors and shapes in (30), towards which the style of (35) is already moving. The model for (35), Juliette Huet, gave birth to a child by Gauguin after his departure for Tahiti.

36. *Vahine No Te Tiare (Woman with Flower).* 1891. Oil. Carlsberg Glypototek, Copenhagen. This picture was the Paris public's first glimpse of Gauguin's Tahitian works. Its surprisingly staid character was perhaps intended to attract portrait commissions; at any rate it aroused little stir.

37. *The Repast.* 1891. Oil. The Louvre, Paris. There are clear echoes of Cézanne in the arrangement of tablecloth, knife and fruit in the foreground. The children, presented like busts and treated like inanimate objects, seem merely to be an extension of the still-life.

38. *Tahitian Mountains.* 1891. Oil. Institute of Arts, Minneapolis. Contrary to popular belief, the mountains were highly inaccessible and a severe barrier to communication on the island. Wild bananas, such as the man carries,

grew there, but lacking the necessary skill to obtain these and other native foods raw, Gauguin resorted to tinned and synthetic foods bought at a local store.

39. *Street in Tahiti.* 1891. Oil. Museum of Art, Toledo. Strong diagonal hatching strokes indicate a partial reversion to a style of 1888–9 (see 11). The disconsolate seated figure adds a touch of melancholy to an otherwise typical mountain landscape.

40. *Man with an Axe.* 1891. Oil. Private Collection, New York. In *Noa Noa* Gauguin describes the scene: "It is morning . . . with a harmonious and subtle gesture the man raises with his two hands a heavy axe which leaves a blue mark against the silvery sky and—below—its incision on the dead tree. . . . On the purple soil long serpentine leaves of a metallic yellow seemed to me like the written characters of a faraway language. . . . In the pirogue the woman was arranging some nets." The figure of the man is derived from a photograph of a Parthenon frieze figure.

41. *Rêverie.* 1891. Oil. William Rockhill Nelson Art Gallery, Kansas City. The daydream was recognized by Baudelaire as a means of perceiving "a sur-reality of which our stable universe is only the simplification, and, so to speak, the caricature." Gauguin and contemporary literary circles in Paris, in which he mixed in 1890–91, were strongly influenced by Baudelaire's ideas (see Note 71).

42. *Tahitian Women Bathing.* 1891–92. Oil. Private Collection, New York. In contrast with the delicately modelled colors of (38) or (39) this picture relies for its effect on large areas of strong but uniform color knitted together by rhythmic arabesques. The bright internal lighting of the picture is a feature which prefigures certain works by the Fauves.

43. *I Raro Te Oviri (Under the Pandanus).* 1891. Oil. Institute of Art, Minneapolis. Again, owing much to the Javanese frieze mentioned above (34), this picture has the flatness of a tapestry through which ripples the strong rhythm of the yellow leaves (40).

44. *Bunch of Flowers.* c. 1900? Oil. Private Collection (New York?).

The exoticism of this tropical flower piece is increased by the mask in the background and the decoration on the vase.

45. *Te Aa No Areois* (*Root of the Ariois*). 1892. Oil. Private Collection, New York. The figure is based on Puvis de Chavannes' picture of Hope (1871), but stylized in the manner of an ancient Egyptian mural of the 18th dynasty. It represents Vairaumati, a famous beauty, as mother of a secret society, long since vanished in Tahiti. The root, a coconut germ, apparently symbolizes the son Vairaumati had by the Tahitian god Oro. Gauguin's mythological information was drawn eclectically from an inaccurate account written some 50 years previously.

46. *Vahine No Te Vi* (*Woman with Mango*). 1892. Oil. Museum of Art, Baltimore. A contorted but flattened composition closely imitates the schema of a Japanese print, most noticeably in the sharp asymmetrical balance of the figure and the long downward curl of the drapery.

47. *Manao Tupapau* (*The Spirit of the Dead Watches*). 1892. Oil. Private Collection, U.S.A. The picture was inspired by an incident on his honeymoon with his Tahitian bride, whom he once found terror-stricken in his hut because the light had gone out. His explanation reveals his artistic intentions: "The Musical part: undulating horizontal lines, harmonies of orange and blue, brought together by yellows and purples. . . . The Literary part: the spirit of the dead. Day and Night."

48. *Parahi Te Marae* (*There is the Temple*). 1892. Oil. Private Collection, U.S.A. Described in a letter to his wife as "the place reserved for the cult of the gods, and for human sacrifices," this scene is largely the product of his own imagination. Tahiti had been thoroughly Europeanized long before and hardly any pagan remains were to be found. In attempting to recapture its past Gauguin created figures and objects derived from Javanese, Egyptian, and other South Pacific cultures.

49. *Te Nave Nave Fenua* (*Land of Delight*). 1892. Oil. Ohara Museum,

Kurashiki, Japan. Gauguin himself once quoted this description by a contemporary critic: "A fantastic garden offers its tempting blooms to the desire of an Edenic Eve who timidly stretches out her hand to pluck the flower of evil while the red wings of the Chimaera flutter whispering on her temples."

50. *Fatate Te Miti* (*By the Sea*). 1892. Oil. National Gallery, Washington, D.C. Perhaps the most lyrical of his first Tahitian paintings, this fully reflects the idyllic life popularly associated with Tahiti. The moving image of the woman entering the waves with uplifted arms occurs elsewhere (4, 90). Here, as elsewhere, the musical sound of the title in Tahitian, of which Gauguin understood little, is used to enhance the exotic appeal.

51. *Head of a Tahitian Woman.* 1891. Ink and water-colors. Private Collection, New York. Even in this sketch, Gauguin's attempt to penetrate the mystery behind the Tahitian countenance is apparent. Despite the delicate modelling of the face, the flat, simple treatment of her hair against the decorative stippling of the background suggests the style of a Japanese print.

52. *Matamoe* (*Landscape with Peacocks*). 1892. Oil. The Hermitage, Leningrad. The peacocks heighten the exoticism of this landscape, which looks through to Tahiti's mountainous interior. For the figure with the axe see (40); it is another example of Gauguin's habit of repeating identical poses in different contexts.

53. *Hina Maruru* (*The Feast of Hina*). 1893. Woodcut, retouched with water-color. This was used as an illustration for *Noa Noa*. The figure is not authentic, but owes something to the shape of ancient stone figures once relatively common on Tahiti, something to the profiles of an ancient Egyptian mural (45), and perhaps something to the mysterious heads of Odilon Redon. In size they are comparable to the tall statues of Easter Island, which he knew about. Rejecting established principles of the woodcut, Gauguin used delicate engraving techniques to produce sparkling semitones by means of dots and lines.

54. *Old Man with Stick.* 1889? Oil. Musée de la Ville de Paris. The

sitter is said to be the impoverished handyman at Marie Henry's inn, where Gauguin stayed in the winter of 1889–90. The subject is simply but firmly painted, and its treatment shows a sympathy and understanding reminiscent of Van Gogh.

55. *Aita Tamari Vahina Judith Te Parari.* 1893. Oil. Private Collection, Berne. His uncle's bequest of 13,000 francs enabled Gauguin to afford several luxuries, including a mistress, Anna, who is pictured here. In his atelier were several exotic objects, a parrot, and a monkey belonging to Anna.

56. *Self-Portrait with Palette.* c. 1891. Oil. Private Collection. A tired face with pockets under the eyes and unkempt long hair sums up Gauguin's career hitherto, a career of frustration and rebellion. The impression is strengthened by the fiery red background.

57. *Portrait of the Artist's Mother.* 1890? Oil. Staatsgalerie, Stuttgart. Undoubtedly this was painted after a photograph, since his mother died in 1867. He retained a tender affection for her. Her face with eyes "so soft and imperious, so pure and caressing," as he described her, appeared as the face of Eve in Paradise in a picture of 1890 painted just before he left for Tahiti.

58. *Hina Te Fatou (The Moon and the Earth).* 1893. Oil. Museum of Modern Art, New York. Gauguin interpreted the Tahitian legend of Hina and Te Fatou in his own terms, distilling from it a deep philosophical truth: the moon, representing matter, is extinguished only to be born again, but man dies never to be reborn.

59. *Pape Moe (Mysterious Waters).* 1893. Oil. Private Collection, Zürich. Enriching with mysterious forms and evocative colors a subject originally taken directly from a photograph, Gauguin made this picture an illustration of a strange incident described in *Noa Noa.* The young girl, surprised at the spring by Gauguin, dove into the pool and was transformed into an eel.

60. *The Siesta.* 1894. Oil. Private Collection, New York. Gauguin has here described a typical Tahitian scene in which the European influence in Tahiti

is all too apparent, both in the manner of dress and in the use of a coal-heated iron.

61. *Mahana No Atua (Day of the God)*. 1894. Oil. Art Institute of Chicago. Painted in Brittany on his return in 1894, such a picture helped to keep alive memories of a romantic Tahiti. By contrast with (60) the scene has a distinct lack of reality, accentuated by the strange colors and shapes of the foreground reflections and by the formality of the composition. It is dominated by the figure of the god Hina, set at the top of its central axis.

62. *Te Arii Vahine (The Queen of Beauty)*. 1896. Water-color. Private Collection, New York. The figure of the reclining queen is no less than Manet's *Olympia*, which Gauguin had copied three years previously, and now transported to a tropical land. In a composition of appropriate formality, the oblique lines are punctuated by the rhythm of the descending verticals. (See also Note 45.) Gauguin told Daniel de Monfreid it represented "the Queen of Beauty in her Edenic setting. The fan signifies ancient nobility, and the mangoes, Tahitian fruit, in the foreground, recall the fruit of Eve."

63. *No Te Aha Oe Riri (Why Are You Angry?)*. 1896. Oil. Art Institute of Chicago. The title intentionally introduces a mood into a picture which otherwise simply and colorfully describes a local scene.

64. *Nave Nave Mahana (Days of Delight)*. 1896. Oil. Musée des Beaux-Arts, Lyon. The monumental and static quality of this picture is very reminiscent of Puvis de Chavannes. Just as his pictures evoke rather than describe antiquity, so do Gauguin's, but in an exotic rather than an archaic context. One is reminded of the words of a Turkish painter's manuscript he owned: "Let all you do bear the imprint of repose and tranquility. Avoid, therefore, poses in movement. Every figure should be static."

65. *Maternity*. 1899. Oil. Private Collection, New York. In April, 1899, Gauguin's second Tahitian wife, Pau'ura, presented him with a child, featured here with his mother while two other women look on.

66. *Poor Fisherman.* 1896. Oil. Museo de Arte, São Paulo. A Tahitian version of a picture of the same name by Puvis de Chavannes, which Gauguin admired.

67. *Self-Portrait.* 1896. Oil. The Louvre, Paris. The portrait, with head turned to the gloom, foretells the attempt at suicide which Gauguin, burdened by severe illness and lack of money, made shortly afterwards. Daniel de Monfreid, to whom the work is dedicated, remained a faithful friend until his death.

68. *Where Have We Come From? What Are We? Where Are We Going?* 1897. Oil on sackcloth. Museum of Fine Arts, Boston. Gauguin painted this spiritual testament shortly before he attempted suicide. The picture reads from right to left. The theme is that of birth, life, and death, but with a philosophical reflection on the innocence of man before his taste of the tree of knowledge caused him to ask these three questions. The fact that studies for many of the figures had been used in previous paintings (see 17, 31, 59, 61) throws doubt on his claim to have painted it spontaneously and in a short space of time, despite its rude execution on an improvised canvas.

69. *Te Tamari No Atua (The Birth of Christ).* 1896. Oil. Bayerische Staatsgemäldesammlungen, Munich. Pau'ura's first child, born at Christmas, became the subject of this Nativity. In the background Gauguin has painted two of his own earlier pictures, divided by the post. The right hand picture closely follows a stable scene by Tassaert of 1857, once in the Arosa Collection. In the general composition of the whole there are echoes of (47).

70. *Portrait of a Young Girl.* 1896. Oil. Museum of Ordrupgaard, Copenhagen. The island's lawyer Goupil commissioned this as a result of a temporary friendship with Gauguin. Unwilling to sit himself, he offered one of his daughters as a sitter. Her youthful innocence has been caught with charming delicacy.

71. *Te Rerioa (The Daydream).* 1897. Oil. Courtauld Institute of Art, London. It is probably the interior of his own house in which the scene takes place. He described the painting: "Everything is dream-like in this picture; is it

the mother, is it the horseman on the track, or better still, is it the dream of the painter!!! All that has nothing to do with painting, people will say. Perhaps, but perhaps not."

72. *Nevermore, O Tahiti.* 1897. Oil. Courtauld Institute of Art, London. This picture, acquired by the composer Delius in 1898, is another which Gauguin himself described: "I wanted by means of a simple nude to suggest a certain barbaric luxury of former times. The whole is drowned in colors deliberately sombre and sad. . . . For title, Nevermore; not the raven of Edgar Poe, but the bird of the devil that is keeping watch."

73. *Vairumati.* 1897. Oil. The Louvre, Paris. In *Noa Noa,* Vairaumati (which Gauguin spelled Vairumati) is poetically described as "a woman of tall stature with the fire of the sun shining in her golden flesh, while all the mysteries of love slumber in the night of her hair." A commonly used image (17, 60, 68) is given majestic effect by placing the head at the apex of the composition (see also 45).

74. *The White Horse.* 1898. Oil. The Louvre, Paris. Transposed coloring brings this close to Fauve pictures, but Gauguin explained it as the result of the play of light in nature during the late afternoon. The gayness of the subject and its interpretation make it seem like a fleeting glimpse of Arcadia. The horse, again taken from an antique model, and of a color with special associations in Tahiti, may embody a synthesis of ancient Western and Polynesian tradition.

75. *Faa Iheihe (Tahitian Pastoral).* 1898. Oil. Tate Gallery, London. During a brief spell of optimism, Gauguin painted what has been regarded as the counterpart to (68), although it is without allegorical content. It comprises a series of festive scenes lacking spatial connection but fused into a joyous image by a shimmering yellow. The format has affinities with the Javanese frieze at Borobodur, and the figures echo the style of Egyptian painting, the Parthenon frieze and Puvis de Chavannes. (See Notes 34, 45, 48.)

76. *Still-Life with Exotic Birds.* 1902. Oil. The Hermitage, Leningrad. See Note 77.

77. *Still-Life with "Hope."* 1901. Oil. Private Collection, Chicago. See also Plate 76. The two pictures have strong associations. The first recalls Cézanne's still-lifes, but is surveyed by a figure of a Buddha, similar to (93), which presumably symbolizes Gauguin's own Buddhist beliefs. He once said of Cézanne himself that he had an "essentially Oriental nature." In the second, a photograph, middle left, recalls Degas, while above it is a version of Puvis de Chavannes' *Hope* of 1871, of which Gauguin had a reproduction. Like the art of Cézanne, that of Puvis appealed to him as an alternative to Impressionism. In the vase are discernible two figures derived from a Marquesan ornament.

78. *The Call.* 1902. Oil. Museum of Art, Cleveland. The figure on the right seems to be based on a figure from the Parthenon frieze of which Gauguin possessed a photograph (see Note 40). The beckoning gesture implies a relationship with something outside the picture and thus renders it at once mysterious and enigmatic.

79. *Barbaric Tales.* 1902. Oil. Folkwang Museum, Essen. In the Marquesas Islands Gauguin found himself surrounded by a wilder environment and a people more savage than in Tahiti. The Satanic figure of Meyer de Haan, recalled from Brittany days, is introduced to intensify the effect of barbaric mysticism (see 31).

80. *The Offering.* 1902. Oil. Private Collection, Zürich. The woman on the left displays marked Mongoloid features in contrast with the almost European features of many Tahitians and Marquesans. Their accurate rendering is evidence of Gauguin's ability to distinguish different racial types. The scene as a whole has Biblical overtones.

81. *The Sorcerer of Hivaoa.* 1902. Oil. Musée des Beaux-Arts, Liège. An impression of a magic aura which seems to surround the sorcerer is conveyed by the depiction of two figures from *The Call* (78), the strange rendering of dog and bird (see 73 and 68), and the luminous intensity of his red cloak.

82. *Horsemen on the Beach.* 1902. Oil. Folkwang Museum, Essen. Again comparatively wealthy, Gauguin was able to enjoy life once more. The effect of

the vanishing riders set against a wide expanse of gay pink reflects a mood matched only in the idyllic days of his first trip to Tahiti. In the distance, however, lurks the hooded figure of Death, a symbol inspired by an engraving by Dürer.

83. *The Last Portrait of Gauguin*. 1903. Oil. Kunstmuseum, Basle. Once attributed to a pupil, this work is now established as the portrait given to Ky Dong, an Annamese prince, in return for his kindness in nursing the sick Gauguin. The artist's increasing illness and the strain of fighting a court action, discernible in the weary expression of his face, soon proved too much for him.

84. *Village Beneath the Snow*. 1899? Oil. The Louvre, Paris. This unfinished landscape of Brittany was found in Gauguin's house after his death. He seems to have retained it for sentimental reasons.

85. *Portrait of Clovis*. 1882? Head of wax on torso of walnut. Private Collection, Paris. The bust was exhibited in the Impressionist Exhibition of 1882. In the previous year Degas had shown a painted wax figure of a young dancer. This bust has none of Degas's concern for casual movement but nonetheless shows a distinct tendency away from the academic finesse and realism of Gauguin's earlier marble portrait of Mette, executed under the influence of the sculptor Bouillot.

86. *Pot Decorated with Figure of a Breton Woman*. 1888–89. Unglazed stoneware. As in his woodcuts, Gauguin revitalized the medium of ceramics by infusing into it a new technique. Instead of being turned on the wheel, his pots are modelled by hand. The figure of the woman sharply bent over appears several times in his sketchbook of this period.

87. *Pot with a Mask*. 1886. Glazed stoneware. Private Collection, Paris. Gauguin learned the art of ceramics from Chaplet, whose hand is evident in the experimental glazing of this pot. Despite the unsuccessful result, Gauguin gave the pot a striking effect by adding gold outlines to the shapes produced by an imperfect glaze. The form of the pot owes a good deal to Peruvian pots with

which Gauguin was familiar from a number in Arosa's possession, those his mother brought back from Peru, and another private collection in Paris.

88. *Carved Wine Barrel.* c. 1889. Marlborough Fine Art Ltd., London. A contemporary writer observed of Gauguin: "He made use of wood, clay, paper, canvas, wall, anything on which to record his ideas and the results of his observations." On the barrel he has carved a playful sequence of Breton subjects.

89. *Be in Love and You will be Happy.* 1889. Linden wood. Museum of Fine Arts, Boston. In this highly finished work, Gauguin deals with the theme of freedom in love. Embittered by the failure of his career and his own personal relationships, he communicates a sarcastic message through erotic symbols. Spatial ambiguities give an uneasy effect.

90. *Be Mysterious.* 1890. Linden wood. Private Collection, Béziers. This panel is an evident counterpart to the former, and apparently deals with the theme of the duality of matter and spirit, although its exact meaning is obscure. "Mystery" was one of the key words in the literary circles amongst whom Gauguin moved in 1890–91.

91. *Hina and Te Fatou.* 1892–93. Tamanu wood. Private Collection. By the deliberately crude finish of this and other Tahitian carvings, Gauguin hoped to convey a spirit of primitiveness. Many of the details are taken from the decoration of Marquesan carved objects but their use is arbitrary and not typical. Because the Tahitians never represented their gods, Gauguin was obliged to use figures of his own creation. See also (58).

92. *L'Après-Midi d'un Faune.* 1891. Tamanu wood. Gauguin made his debt to the Symbolist poets explicit in this carving in which he substituted his own version of the idyll of the poet Mallarmé that was set to music by Debussy. Talking of his own paintings of Tahitians, Gauguin once quoted from the idyll, "These nymphs, I want to perpetuate them. . . ."

93. *Idol with Pearl.* 1892–93. Tamanu wood. Private Collection. Believ-

ing in the essential unity of all religions, Gauguin felt free to confuse Buddhist and Tahitian imagery, as he does here. For this reason allusions to Buddhism are also common elsewhere (see 76).

94. *Idol with Shell.* 1893. Ironwood. Private Collection. Gauguin has created a mysterious amalgam of Buddhist, Marquesan and Tahitian elements. The Buddha figure (cf. 93) has been transformed by the adoption of traditional Marquesan stylized motifs for the feet and legs. Shell is commonly used in the South Pacific for ornaments and utensils.

95. *Section of Carved Door Frame.* 1901. Redwood. The Louvre, Paris. This panel formed part of the large door frame of his Marquesan house, and issued to all incomers the directions inscribed on the two earlier woodcarvings done in Brittany (89, 90). In a land celebrated for sensual pleasure and mysterious enchantment, the sentiments are particularly appropriate. The tradition of carved panels around the housefront belongs more properly to the Maori house of New Zealand.

96. *Te Fare Amu (The Dining Room).* 1901? Redwood. Private Collection, New York. Probably the dining-room of his Tahitian house. The face of the right hand figure is clearly derived from the traditional stylization of the Marquesan face. In both this and the former the wood is cut away in shallow relief, to emphasize the linear quality of the design. Gauguin sometimes even recut his woodcuts to produce bas-reliefs like these.

THE PLATES

1 *Gauguin Before his Easel.* 1885. Oil. 25⅝ × 21⅜ in. Private Collection, Berne. Gauguin takes his stance as a competent painter, fully conversant with Impressionist technique.

2 *Still-Life in an Interior.* 1885. Oil. 23½ × 29¼ in. Private Collection, U.S.A. Pictorial ambiguity is achieved by the use of double perspective.

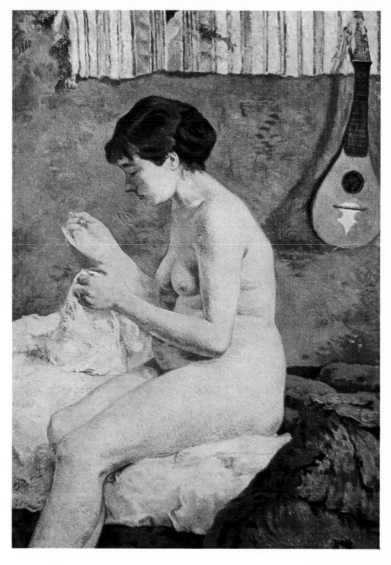

3 *Study of a Nude.*   1880.   Oil.   45¼ × 31½ in.   Ny Carlsberg Glyptotek, Copenhagen.   The realism of the nude is very much in the tradition of Courbet.

4 *The Beach at Dieppe*. 1885. Oil. 28⅛ × 28⅛ in. Ny Carlsberg Glyptotek, Copenhagen. The bright atmosphere of the coast in true Impressionist style.

5 *Cows by the Seaside*.   1886.   Oil.   29½ × 44⅛ in.   Private Collection.   Gauguin's first
contact with the ruggedness of Brittany.

6 *Four Breton Women.* **1886.** Oil. **28⅜ × 35⅞** in. Bayerische Staatsgemäldesammlungen, Munich. The strange shapes of the native costume fascinated Gauguin.

7 *Two Women from Martinique.* 1887. Charcoal and pastel. (Present whereabouts unknown.)
A fine description of the ponderous form of the Negress.

8 *Vision After the Sermon* or *Jacob Wrestling with the Angel.* 1888. Oil. 28¾ × 36¼ in. National Gallery of Scotland, Edinburgh. The color and style mark the birth of Synthetism.

9
Still-Life with Three Puppies. 1888. Oil. 36¼ × 25⅝ in. Museum of Modern Art, New York. A daring experiment in combining pictorially motifs unrelated in space.

10 *Landscape with Cows.* 1889. Water-color. 10⅜ × 12½ in. Private Collection, New York. A very flat composition despite extreme foreshortening.

11 *Les Alyscamps, Arles.* 1888. Oil. 36¼ × 28¾ in. The Louvre, Paris. The weft of small diagonally directed strokes shows a clear debt to Cézanne.

12 *Woman with Pitcher, Pont-Aven.* 1888. Oil. 36¼ × 28⅜ in. Private Collection, New York. An intensely personal interpretation of the Brittany landscape.

13 *Old Women of Arles*. 1888. Oil. 28¾ × 36¼ in. Art Institute of Chicago. Perspective distortions and simplified color distinguish this from Van Gogh's version.

14 *Among the Lilies, Brittany*.   1889.   Oil.   36¼ × 28¾ in.   Kunstmuseum, Basle.   An in-
stance of Gauguin's adaptation of motives from other artists' work—here, Courbet's dog.

15 *Haymaking.* 1889. Oil. 36¼ × 28¾ in. Courtauld Institute of Art, London. The swirling composition is appropriate to the activity of harvesting.

16 *La Belle Angèle*.   1889.   Oil.   36¼ × 28⅜ in.   The Louvre, Paris.   A portrait of the keeper of a local café.

17 *Women Gathering Seaweed.* 1889. Oil. 34½ × 48⅜ in. Folkwang Museum, Essen. The picture is pervaded by a mood of desolation strongly felt by Gauguin himself.

18 *Young Breton Girls by the Sea.* 1889. Oil. 36¼ × 28¾ in. National Museum of Western
Art, Tokyo. An unusually sentimental picture of two girls in traditional costume.

19 *Still-Life with Fan*. 1889. Oil. 19¾ × 24 in. The Louvre, Paris. This incorporates elements drawn from Cézanne and from Gauguin's ceramics.

20　*The Green Christ*.　1889.　Oil.　36¼ × 28¾ in.　Musées Royaux des Beaux-Arts de Belgique, Brussels.　Sombre coloring in a composition with strong symbolic overtones.

21 *Christ in the Garden of Olives.* 1889. Oil. 36⅝ × 29⅛ in. Norton Gallery, West Palm Beach. Depressed and feeling betrayed, Gauguin portrays himself in the image of Christ.

22 *The Yellow Christ*. 1889. Oil. 36¼ × 28¾ in. Albright-Knox Art Gallery, Buffalo. Another religious work in which the crucifix symbolizes Gauguin's own suffering.

23 *Self-Portrait with the Yellow Christ.* **1889.** Oil. 15 × 18⅛ in. Private Collection. A searching self-portrait with strong emotive content.

24 *Self-Portrait as a Symbolist.* 1889. Oil on wood. 31¼ × 20¼ in. National Gallery, Washington, D.C. The halo, serpent, and apples indicate a preoccupation with Satanism.

25 *Still-Life with Ham.* 1889. Oil. 19¾ × 22⅞ in. Phillips Gallery, Washington, D. C. Emphatic verticals of the background hold the pictorial balance.

26 *Still-Life with Japanese Print*.   1889.   Oil.   28¾ × 36¼ in.   Private Collection, New York.
A bright still-life whose rhythmic disposition in horizontal bands may be compared with (37).

27 *The Schuffenecker Family.* 1889. Oil. 28¾ × 36¼ in. The Louvre, Paris. Gauguin was often aided materially by his painter friend Schuffenecker.

28 *Madeleine Bernard.* 1888. Oil. 28⅜ × 22⅞ in. Musée des Beaux-Arts, Grenoble. Degas is the inspiration behind this pensive portrait of Émile Bernard's sister.

29 *Les Folies de l'Amour.* 1890. Gouache. 10½ in., diameter. Private Collection. Some esoteric symbols of love, playfully presented.

30 *Harvest By the Sea*.   1890.   Oil.   28¾ × 36¼ in.   Private Collection, London.   An increasing schematization of landscape forms.

31 *Nirvana: Portrait of Meyer de Haan.*   1889.   Oil and turpentine on silk.   8 × 11⅛ in.
Wadsworth Atheneum, Hartford.   A mysterious melancholy induced by charged images.

32 *The Field of Potatoes.* 1890. Oil. 28¾ × 36¼ in. Private Collection, New York. The bright, gay colors presage his early Tahitian pictures.

33 *Two Tahitian Women on the Beach.* 1891. Oil. 27⅛ × 35⅞ in. The Louvre, Paris. The bronzed and languid forms of Tahitian women.

34 *Ia Orana Maria.* 1891. Oil. 44⅞ × 35 in. Metropolitan Museum of Art, New York. An interpretation of a Christian theme in Tahitian terms.

35 *The Loss of Virginity.* 1890–91. Oil. 35⅜ × 51⅛ in. Chrysler Art Museum, Provincetown. The effect of Gauguin's contact with literary circles in Paris.

36 *Vahine No Te Tiare* (*Woman with Flower*). 1891. Oil. 27¾ × 18¼ in.   Ny Carlsberg-Glyptotek, Copenhagen.   His first Tahitian picture to be exhibited in Paris.

37 *The Repast.* 1891. Oil. 28¾ × 36¼ in. The Louvre, Paris. A typically Tahitian still-life with echoes of Cézanne.

38 *Tahitian Mountains.* 1891. Oil. 26¾ × 36⅜ in. Institute of Arts, Minneapolis. The mountainous interior, inaccessible to Europeans.

39 *Street in Tahiti*. 1891. Oil. 45½ × 34¼ in. Museum of Art, Toledo. Typical mountain
landscape tinged with melancholy by the disconsolate seated figure.

40 *Man with an Axe*. 1891. Oil. 36¼ × 27½ in. Private Collection, New York. Rarely had Gauguin dared to juxtapose such pungent colors as he did now.

41 *Rêverie*.   1891.   Oil.   37⅜ × 26¾ in.   William Rockhill Nelson Art Gallery, Kansas City.
The dream-like trance in which some of Gauguin's own pictures were reportedly conceived.

42 *Tahitian Women Bathing.*   1891–92.   Oil.   43⅜ × 35⅛ in.   Private Collection, New York.
Flat areas of simplified color give the picture its own internal lighting.

43 *I Raro Te Oviri* (*Under the Pandanus*). 1891. Oil 28⅜ × 36 in. Institute of Art, Minneapolis.   The long yellow leaves infuse a rippling rhythm.

44 *Bunch of Flowers.* c. 1900? Oil. 37⅜ × 24⅜ in. Private Collection (New York?). A highly exotic flower painting.

45 *Te Aa No Areois* (*Root of the Ariois*). 1892. Oil. 36¼ × 28¾ in. Private Collection, New York. A stylized rendering of a Tahitian mythological figure.

46 *Vahine No Te Vi (Woman with Mango).* 1892. Oil. 27¼ × 17½ in. Museum of Art, Baltimore. The composition closely imitates the schema of a Japanese print.

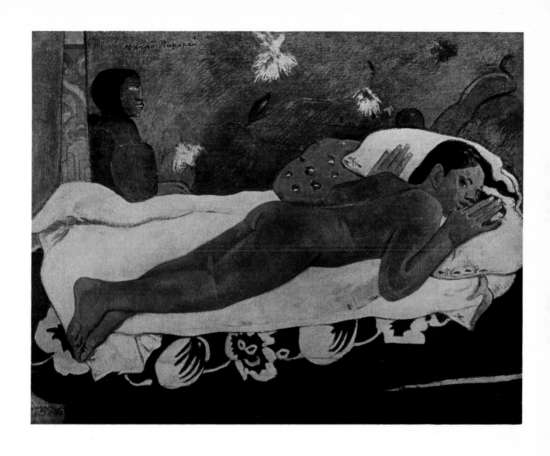

47 *Manao Tupapau* (*The Spirit of the Dead Watches*). 1892. Oil. 28¾ × 36¼ in. Private Collection, U.S.A. A painting inspired by his Tahitian wife's fear of the dark.

48 *Parahi Te Marae (There is the Temple).* 1892. Oil. 26¾ × 35⅞ in. Private Collection, U.S.A. Gauguin's recreation of Tahiti's pagan past was largely imaginative.

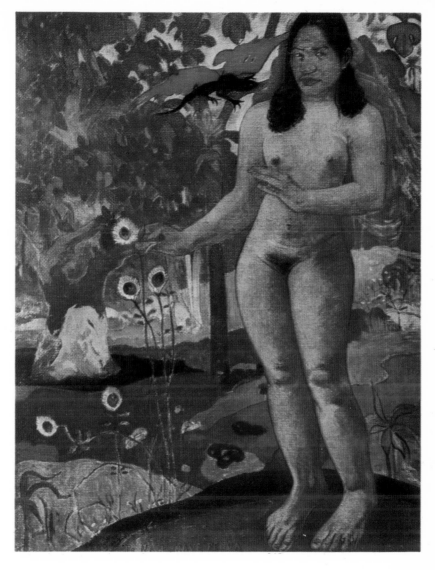

49 *Te Nave Nave Fenua (Land of Delight)*. 1892. Oil. 36 × 28½ in. Ohara Museum, Kura-shiki, Japan. An Edenic Eve timidly stretches out her hand to pluck the flower of evil.

50 *Fatata Te Miti (By the Sea).* 1892. Oil. 26¾ × 36 in. National Gallery, Washington, D.C. A lyrical expression of the idyllic life popularly associated with Tahiti.

Inconnu de Paul Gauguin. Emile Bernard. 29

Gauguin

51 *Head of a Tahitian Woman.* 1891. Ink and water-colors. 10 × 12 in. Private Collection,
New York. Even in this sketch, the mystery of the Tahitian countenance is probed.

52 *Matamoe (Landscape with Peacocks)*.   1892.   Oil.   45¼ × 37⅞ in.   The Hermitage, Leningrad.   Peacocks enhance the exotic appeal of the mountain landscape.

53 *Hina Maruru (The Feast of Hina).* 1893. Woodcut, retouched with water-color. 6½ × 5⅜ in. The use of delicate engraving techniques produced sparkling semitones.

54
Old Man with Stick.
1889? Oil. 27½ ×
17¾ in. Musée de
la Ville de Paris.
The sympathetic
treatment of the
subject is reminis-
cent of Van Gogh.

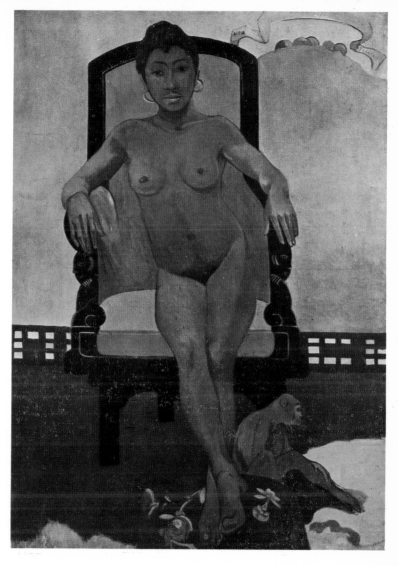

55 *Aita Tamari Vahina Judith Te Parari.* 1893. Oil. 46 × 32½ in. Private Collection, Berne. The bright colors of Tahiti continue in Paris.

56 *Self-Portrait with Palette.* c. 1891. Oil. 21⅝ × 18⅛ in. Private Collection. The tired face of a rebel painter.

57 *Portrait of the Artist's Mother*. 1890? Oil. 16⅛ × 13 in. Staatsgalerie. Stuttgart. Testimony to the tender affection Gauguin felt for his mother.

58 *Hina Te Fatou (The Moon and the Earth).* 1893. Oil. 44⅛ × 24⅜ in. Museum of Modern Art, New York. The Gods of Moon and Earth in sacred conversation.

59 *Pape Moe (Mysterious Waters).* 1893. Oil. 39 × 29½ in. Private Collection, Zürich.
Strange forms and evocative colors add mystery to this scene.

60 *The Siesta*. 1894. Oil. 34¼ × 45⅝ in. Private Collection, New York. A frank description of Europeanized Tahiti.

61 *Mahana No Atua (Day of the God)*.   1894.   Oil.   26 × 42½ in.   Art Institute of Chicago.
Strange shapes and colors contrast with the formality of the whole composition.

62 *Te Arii Vahine (The Queen of Beauty)*. 1896. Water-color. 6¾ × 9 in. Private Collection, New York. Manet's *Olympia* transformed into the legendary Tahitian queen.

63 *No Te Aha Oe Riri* (*Why Are You Angry?*).   1896.   Oil.   37⅜ × 51⅛ in.   Art Institute of
Chicago.   The title introduces a mood into a picture of a local scene.

NAVE NAVE MAHANA

64 *Nave Nave Mahana (Days of Delight).* **1896.** Oil. **37 × 51⅛ in.** Musée des Beaux-Arts, Lyon. Monumental, static figures in a tropical Elysium.

65 *Maternity.* 1899. Oil. 36⅜ × 23⅝ in. Private Collection, New York. The birth of a son by his second Tahitian wife inspired this maternity picture.

66 *Poor Fisherman.* 1896. Oil. 29⅞ × 26 in. Museo de Arte, São Paulo. A Tahitian version of a picture by Puvis de Chavannes.

67 *Self-Portrait*. 1896. Oil. 15¾ × 13¾ in. The Louvre, Paris. A gloomy portrait foretelling his attempt at suicide.

68 *Where Have We Come From? What Are We? Where Are We Going?* 1897. Oil on sackcloth. 54¾ × 147¾ in. Museum of Fine Arts, Boston. A monumental picture in which Gauguin's spiritual testament is written in emotive images.

69 *Te Tamari No Atua (The Birth of Christ)*. 1896. Oil. 37¾ × 50⅜ in. Bayerische Staatsgemäldesammlungen, Munich. The birth of his own child at Christmas inspired this Nativity.
70 *Portrait of a Young Girl*. 1896. Oil. 29½ × 25⅝ in. Museum of Ordrupgaard, Copenhagen. Youthful innocence painted with charm and delicacy.

71 *Te Rerioa (The Daydream)*. 1897. Oil. 37⅜ × 52 in. Courtauld Institute of Art, London.
A dream-like state is suggested.

72 *Nevermore, O Tahiti.* 1897. Oil. 27⅜ × 45⅝ in. Courtauld Institute of Art, London. A nude, drowned in sombre, sad colors, suggests barbaric luxury of former times.

73 *Vairumati.* 1897. Oil. 28¾ × 37 in. The Louvre, Paris. A commonly used image given majestic effect.

74 *The White Horse*. 1898. Oil. 55½ × 35⅞ in. The Louvre, Paris. The play of light in nature during the late afternoon.

75 *Faa Iheihe (Tahitian Pastoral).* 1898. Oil. 21¼ × 66½ in. Tate Gallery, London. A series of festive scenes, spatially unrelated but fused together by a shimmering yellow.

76 *Still-Life with Exotic Birds.* 1902. Oil. 24⅜ × 29⅞ in. The Hermitage, Leningrad. A Buddha figure breathes a spirit of the Orient into a Cézannesque still-life.

77 *Still-Life with "Hope."* 1901. Oil. 25¾ × 30¼ in. Private Collection, Chicago. Tahitian and European associations mingle together.

78 *The Call.* 1902. Oil. 51¼ × 35¼ in. Museum of Art, Cleveland. The gesture renders the picture at once mysterious and enigmatic.

79 *Barbaric Tales*. 1902. Oil. 51⅛ × 35⅜ in. Folkwang Museum, Essen. The Satanic image of de Haan intensifies an effect of barbaric mysticism.

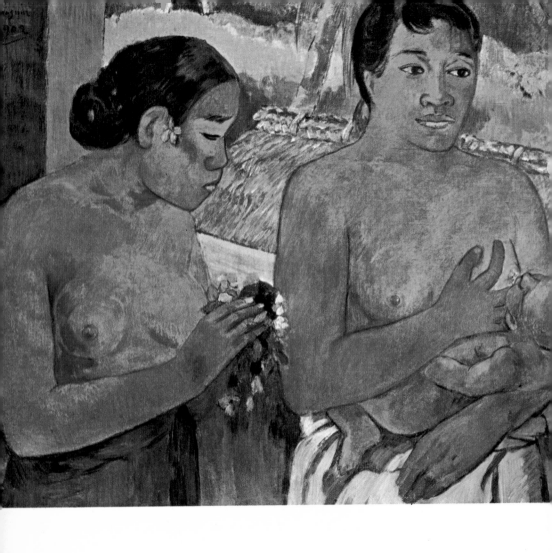

80 *The Offering*. 1902. Oil. 27 × 30⅞ in. Private Collection, Zürich. The accurate rendering of Mongoloid features shows Gauguin's fascination with racial types.

81 *The Sorcerer of Hivaoa.* 1902. Oil. 36¼ × 28¾ in. Musée des Beaux-Arts, Liège. A magic aura seems to surround the sorcerer.

82 *Horsemen on the Beach.* 1902. Oil. 25⅞ × 29⅞ in. Folkwang Museum. Essen. Vanishing riders on the gay pink of the beach reflect an idyllic mood.

83
The Last Portrait of Gauguin. 1903. Oil. 16⅜ ×
9½ in. Kunstmuseum,
Basle. Illness and fatigue,
here discernible, induced his
death soon after.

84 *Village Beneath the Snow.* 1899? Oil. 25⅝ × 35⅜ in. The Louvre, Paris. A sentimental reminder of Brittany.

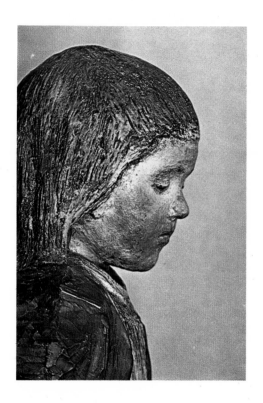

85 *Portrait of Clovis*. 1882? Head of wax on torso of walnut. 15¾ in. Private Collection, Paris. Gauguin moves away from academic finesse and realism.

86 *Pot Decorated with Figure of a Breton Woman.*
1888–89. Unglazed stoneware. h. 5⅛ in. Private
Collection, Paris.

87 *Pot with a Mask.* 1886. Glazed stoneware. h. 7⅝ in. Private Collection,
Paris.

88 *Carved Wine Barrel.*   c. 1889.   l. 14⅝ × dia. 12¼ in.   Marlborough Fine Art Ltd., London.
A playful sequence of Breton subjects.

soyez amoureuses
vous serez
heureuses

← 89 *Be in Love and You will be Happy.* 1889. Linden wood. h. 38¼ × l. 29½ in. Museum of Fine Arts, Boston.   The sarcastic message of an embittered man.

90 *Be Mysterious.* 1890. Linden wood.   h. 28¾ × l. 37⅜ in.   Private Collection, Béziers. Obscure esoteric symbols mingle in this counterpart to (89).

91 *Hina and Te Fatou.* 1892–93. Tamanu
Wood. h. 12⅝ × dia. 5½ in. Private
Collection.

92 *L'Après-Midi d'un Faune.* 1891. Tamanu Wood. h. 13⅜ × w. 4¾ × depth
3½ in. Private Collection, Paris.

94 *Idol with Shell.* 1893. Ironwood. h.
10⅝ × dia. 5½ in. Private Collection.

93 *Idol with Pearl.* 1892–93. Tamanu
Wood. h. 9⅞ in. Private Collection.

95 *Section of Carved Door Frame.* 1901. Redwood. 95½ × 15⅜ in. The Louvre, Paris. The carved entrance panel of New Zealand tradition.

96 *Te Fare Amu (The Dining Room).* 1901? Redwood. l. 58¼ × w. 9⅞ in. Private Collection, New York. The sharply cut shallow relief emphasizes the linear quality.